Short & Sweet

(and f*cking brutal)

Bailee Elaine

DEDICATION

I'd like to say that I wrote this book for my brother, Brady, and my family.

The truth is, as selfish as it may seem, I think I wrote this book for me.

I've come a long way to write this book. I've struggled to find the words; I've struggled to dive deep into the memories that make up this story. I've attempted to write it in poetry and I've attempted to write it narratively. For now, I'll stick with what I know best.

Poetry — simple; short and sweet.

INTRODUCTION

Death is uncomfortable.
This book was not written for comfort.
But you may find crooked solace within it.

Relativity.

Some kind of answers that you've been looking for.
Some kind of truth;
that death is not always beautiful.
And that it is, too.

PART I

On October 9th of 2004, my brother, Brady, died
in an ATV accident.
He was ten, I was six.
And I don't remember a single thing in that year other
than this.

I feel as though some part of me died along with you.
I was so young
and so were you.
I didn't know how to determine the difference between us two.

Maybe I did actually die,
in some way.

I lost sight of myself.
I lost sight of anything true to hold onto.
My heart shattered.

My lights went out.

I remember the silly moments in the wake of chaos.
My mind's way of reminding me that we were just kids.

I can still see the pain on my father's face,
the tears rolling from his eyes.
As he cries from the loss of his oldest son.

I can only imagine the fear in my mother's chest,
as she receives the news from home.
So far away from her baby.

I can't help but to find it unfair.

Unfair,

that strangers got to be with you as you left this world.

Yet, I can't remember the last thing I told you.

"Brady's not coming home this time."
The only words my dad could muster up
to tell his kids their brother had died.

Short and sweet.
And fucking brutal.

A room full of flowers.
Aromatic —
sweet but tangy,
kind of bitter.

The smell of flowers forever tangled in a memory.

My heart breaks for the six year old girl who saw her big brother
lying in a casket, eyes closed, cold.

My heart breaks for the parents who lost their baby boy,
for the fifteen year old girl who lost her little brother,
and the eight year old boy who lost his brother and best friend.

I was afraid to touch you.

I was afraid to say goodbye.

I was afraid to never see you again in this life.

Nobody tells you what it feels like once the funeral is over,
when everyone leaves to go back to their own lives.

Confusion.
Heartbreak.
Disbelief.
Loneliness.
Emptiness.
Silence.

And don't be fooled.
Silence is loud.
Moments, days, weeks —
little to no words to speak.
"When will this end?"

But it doesn't end.
The days go by while you're still here and they're gone.
Just like that,
gone.

And the thing about it all —
The one thing behind the madness, chaos, isolation, the pain;
It's okay.

Your world stops for a moment, or a few.
A lifetime,
at least the world you once knew.
But you keep going.
You find the strength to move forward.

Life isn't over,
yours anyway.
You learn to forgive and love even harder.

It's okay to allow silence to yell,
and to yell over the silence.

"Do you remember him?"

Of course I remember him, that's my brother.

A simple question.

I never knew one could make me feel so small.

It's funny how our brain works with our body
and how our body works with our soul.
How you can lose someone at an age so young —
how you can lose someone at all.
But you remember them through memories, stories, and dreams.
And when those memories start to fade,
and you find yourself questioning existence in its entirety,
you remember them through love.

Letters tied to green balloons.
Hoping they might reach you.

And after that, life went on.

PART II

After years of searching for something or someone

to remind me of you —

I've found a lot of things

and people

and places

that do.

I think of you often.

What you would be like.

The type of person you'd marry.

The things you'd be doing.

I think about the things we would enjoy together.

The things I do now,

where I feel you the most.

I've created a person in my mind of who I thought you might be.

And to know that I'll never meet them in this lifetime

is a bit heartbreaking.

I painted you, I drew you, I wrote you.

I felt you.

I feel you.

And that is the only form in which I truly know you.

Beautiful, undoubtedly.

Yet; to hold you, touch you, hear you, see you —

That is a gift too often taken for granted.

Life seemed perfect once upon a time.

Life has a way of doing that,
showing you just how perfect and imperfect it can be.

That there are ups and downs
and sometimes,
relationships end and people die.

Holidays weren't the same after you left.

Joy turned to sadness.

Smiles turned to tears.

Excitement turned to guilt.

Holidays were just another reminder that you were gone.

I'll never forget the summer you caught my index finger with a fishing hook.

Oh what I'd give to be able to fish with you again.

Please visit me soon.
Either in a dream or as a bird,
I don't care how you do.

But I miss you.

[may 6th, 2009]

I used to think that breakup songs were about death,
because I loved you and I lost you.

I've come to realize
how much my entire existence has revolved around death.
I think about it often,
I fear it often,
I sit with it often.
I feel that it's something I know all too well
and yet, nothing about.

Motor accidents, drug abuse, suicide,
I've lost count.

And you say to me in your condescending manner,
"Do you have any idea what I've been through?"

I might throw up.

It's painful and dark,
this place has broken my heart.

I have no answers for you or for me.
I have no words to explain the uncertainty.

The living must go on
without those who are gone —

Destined to be angels.

Death has since become intriguing.
The darkness feels familiar.
Something that follows me
and something that I seek.

The feeling —
When everything is right,
something must be wrong.

Nostalgic melancholy.

We do our best,

when we experience trauma.

Sometimes our best results in guilt and dissociation.

(Trauma, how sick I am of that word)

Guilt has found its host,
and I still struggle to peel it off my back.

I feel you sometimes.
I know when you're near.
A wave of emotion crashes over me and I can't stop the tears.
I know that it's you.

And sometimes,
months go by
where I don't have a single tear to cry.

Numb.

[The Sand Dunes]

"Have you ever been?"
I swallow my heart,
now my stomach is beating.

That's where my brother died.
Do I say it?

I throw him a sheepish, "yeah."
Trying to hide the memory behind my eyes.

— It's 2am.
I can't sleep.
The tension in my body is screaming.

My heart is in my stomach,
now my stomach is beating.

These conversations of funerals and death.
Where do I fit in?
Too familiar.
Yet, I don't know a damn thing.

The thing is,
grief just wants to be acknowledged.

It wants to be felt.
And once it is, it usually goes away.
It comes back,
but it goes away.

The sadness, the pain, the anxiety,
they're really just our emotions telling us something.

And once we let those emotions be felt,
let them know we are listening —
We create space for them to move through us.

For a long time,
I thought that I had to let you go.
Really, I just had to accept what I already know.

I had to let go of the anger
and the pain.
The guilt
and the shame,
for when I cry tears in your name.

You will be with me forever.

Death confronted me before I knew it's name.
Robbed me of my innocence,
it took the magic of life away.

Both of which feel true,
it showed me beauty too.

Death showed me passion,
as it drained me of emotion.
Love,
as it swallowed me in grief.
Strength,
when all I could feel was weakness.

Death showed me angels —
among us,
within us.
The unseen world around us.

Death confronted me to show me about existence.

Open your heart and your mind
to this unknown world.
You now have an angel watching over you.
Feel them in your heart,
in the sun and in the air.
Although they are gone,
they're not too far from here.

I don't need knives, I've got angels.

So I lie on my floor and cry.
I wonder if they'll ever stop —
the tears.

Although I don't feel so sad at the moment,
I feel everything that once was
f a d i n g

I know that this will forever be a part of me.

And with that in my knowing,
I'll continue to let it go.
I don't need to hold this weight anymore.

With love,
Bai

"Forever young"

ABOUT THE AUTHOR

Bailee Elaine is an author based in Salt Lake City, Utah.

baileeelaine.com

instagram.com/baileeelainewrites

www.ingramcontent.com/pod-product-compliance
Lightning Source LLC
Chambersburg PA
CBHW030525130626
46549CB00007B/3099